SNAP SHOT™

Art director Roger Priddy
Editor Mary Ling
Designer Joanna Pocock
Design assistant Sharon Grant

Model makers
Centaur Studios: Triceratops pp. 8-9,
Iguanodon pp. 24-25. Roby Braun:
Stegosaurus pp. 10-11, Compsognathus pp. 12-13.
John Holmes: Gallimus pp. 28-29,
Hypsilophodon pp. 28-29.

SNAPSHOT™
is an imprint of Covent Garden Books.
232 Madison Avenue,
New York, New York 10016

Copyright © 1994
Covent Garden Books Ltd., London.

2 4 6 8 10 9 7 5 3 1

Color reproduction by Colourscan
Printed in Belgium by Proost

INCREDIBLE
DINOSAURS

Written by
Christopher Maynard

Contents

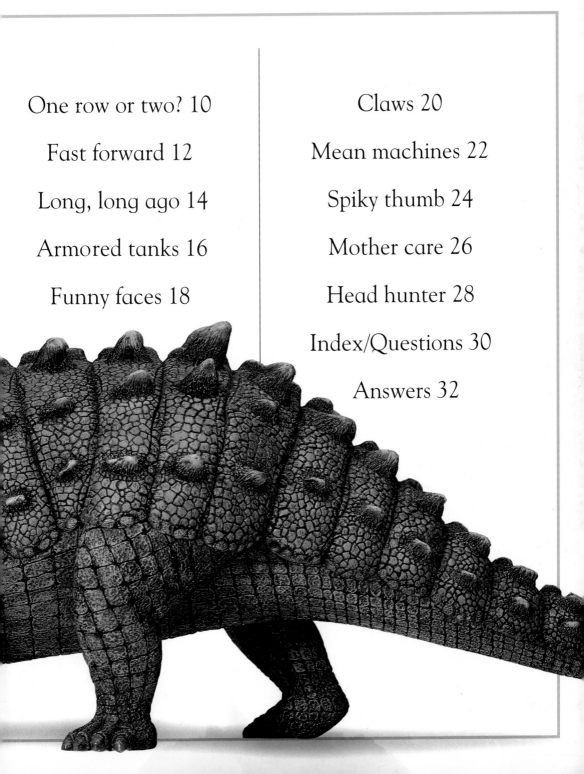

Big tooth

Tyrannosaurus was king of the meat-eaters. It killed its prey with its wicked scooping bite. It even attacked the biggest game, including giants like *Triceratops*.

Serrated tooth

Teeth as big as kitchen knives

Snap! When a tooth broke off, a new one soon grew in its place.

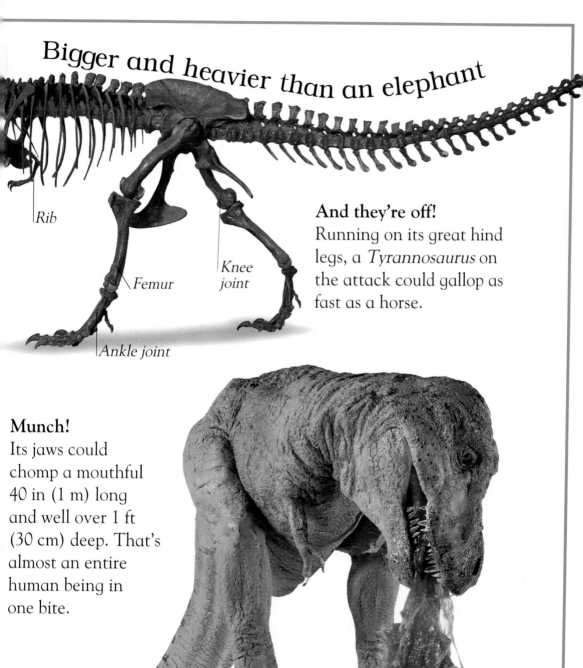

Bigger and heavier than an elephant

Rib

Femur

Knee
joint

Ankle joint

And they're off!
Running on its great hind
legs, a *Tyrannosaurus* on
the attack could gallop as
fast as a horse.

Munch!
Its jaws could
chomp a mouthful
40 in (1 m) long
and well over 1 ft
(30 cm) deep. That's
almost an entire
human being in
one bite.

A head with three horns

Think of an elephant. Then add a hooked beak, huge horns, and a frill of thick bone. What you end up with is a *Triceratops!*

Big frill
When a *Triceratops* lowered its head to charge, the frill made its face look twice as big and dangerous.

It was as much a rhino as a dino

Frill

Brow ho

Nos horr

Heavy head
It would take all your strength to lift a *Triceratops* skull.

Long horn

The twin horns above its eyebrows might grow as long as an adult human being.

Wavy edge of frill

What food did it eat?

othless beak

iceratops used its big hooked parrot's beak to p through tough plants. Behind it were rows of th that sliced up the plants even more.

One row or two?

When the fossils of *Stegosaurus* were first found, dinosaur hunters thought the huge bony plates lay flat on its back. They called it "roofed lizard."

Big eater
Stegosaurus was a plant eater. Because it weighed almost two tons, it spent most of the day grazing on plants to satisfy its huge appetite.

Tilt!
With its shorter front legs and its small head near the ground, it could reach low-growing plants.

10

Wobble
The plates were attached to the skin, not to the skeleton.

Air conditioning
The plates controlled body temperature. When it was hot they gave off heat. When it got cold, they soaked up warmth.

Dorsal plate

Femur

Ulna

Chevron

11

Fast forward

Compsognathus was a tiny dinosaur built for speed. It darted around chasing after small lizards and insects. With its thin legs and birdlike feet, it was a very fast runner.

Stal
It had dozens of tiny razo
sharp teeth

Tiny dino
You could lift *Compsognathus* in one hand. It was no bigger than a chicken.

Eye spy
Like a bird, it had big eyes to help it find and track down small, fast-moving prey.

meat-eating chicken that bites

Jaw muscle

Forelimb

Thigh

Claw

Hallux (first toe)

Fine fossil
Its tiny bones were beautifully preserved in a bed of fine mud. One skeleton even had the remains of its last lizard meal in its stomach.

Long, long ago

From nose to tail, the *Barosaurus* stretched 88 ft (27 m). That's almost as long as a blue whale or three buses!

All neck and tail, with a very tubby tummy

Giants
Barosaurus and its relatives were the biggest animals ever to walk on land. Next to them, a full-grown elephant would look like a baby.

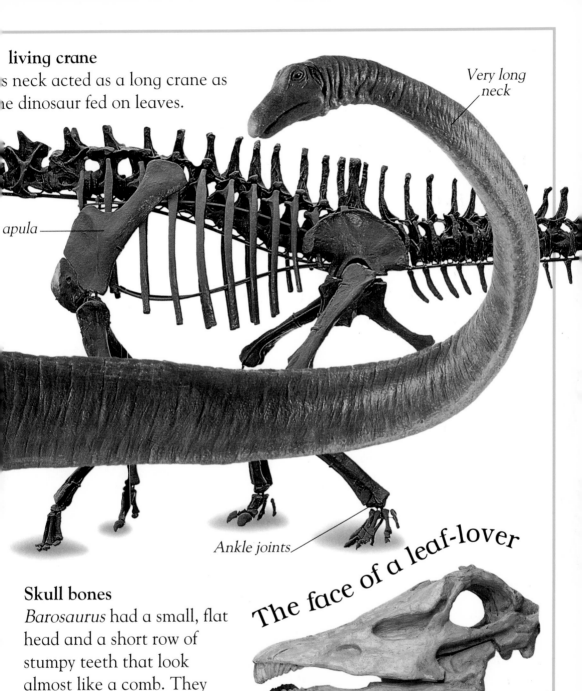

living crane
s neck acted as a long crane as
e dinosaur fed on leaves.

Very long neck

apula

Ankle joints

The face of a leaf-lover

Skull bones
Barosaurus had a small, flat
head and a short row of
stumpy teeth that look
almost like a comb. They
were used to rake leaves from
branches and twigs.

Armored tanks

The most heavily armored dinosaurs of all were the *Ankylosaurs.*
These giants were covered with thick leathery skin, plates of bone, and horny spikes.

Join the club
At the end of its heavy tail were two thick lumps of bone.
They joined together to turn the end of the tail into a dangerous club.

Low blow
Its heavy tail could swing hard from side to side and cripple the legs of any hunter that came too close.

So well armored they never had to run away

Tail club

Shoulder
spike

Armored tail

Hind foot

Slow and low
Really big *Ankylosaurs* might
have weighed three tons or more with all that
heavy armor. But they were only as
tall as your front door!

Bone helmet
Tiny eyes peered out
from under a shield
of bone.

Funny faces

Dinosaurs had strange faces. Horns and knobs stuck out all over the place.

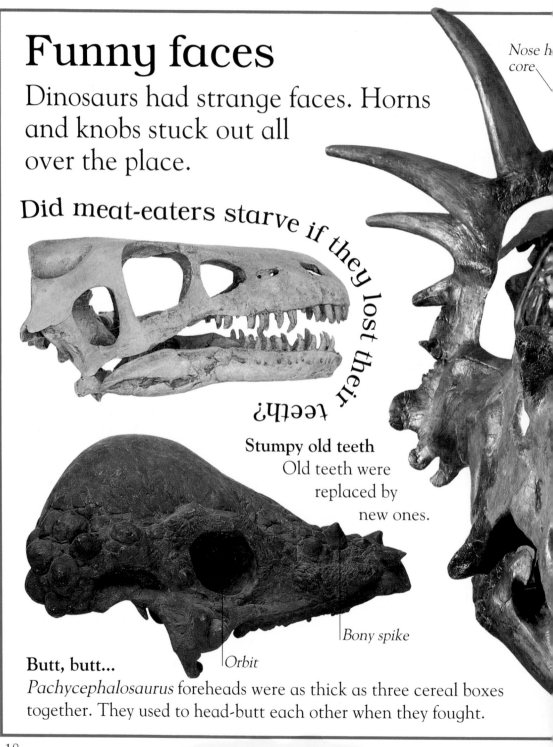

Nose horn
core

Did meat-eaters starve if they lost their teeth?

Stumpy old teeth
Old teeth were replaced by new ones.

Bony spike

Orbit

Butt, butt...
Pachycephalosaurus foreheads were as thick as three cereal boxes together. They used to head-butt each other when they fought.

long horn

Meet Spike!
Styracosaurus had six long spikes poking from its frill. Six short ones and a nose horn completed the set.

Parrot beak
Some plant-eaters, like *Psittacosaurus*, had a great horny beak for cutting leafy food.

Did dinos have underwater snorkels?

Horn-blower
Parasaurolophus had a bony crest on its head as long as a man is tall. The hollow tubes inside made loud honking sounds, but the *Parasaurolophus* couldn't breathe through it.

Claws

In 1982 a giant dinosaur claw was found in a quarry. Its outer curve alone would stretch right across this open book. *Baryonyx* was a big meat-eater.

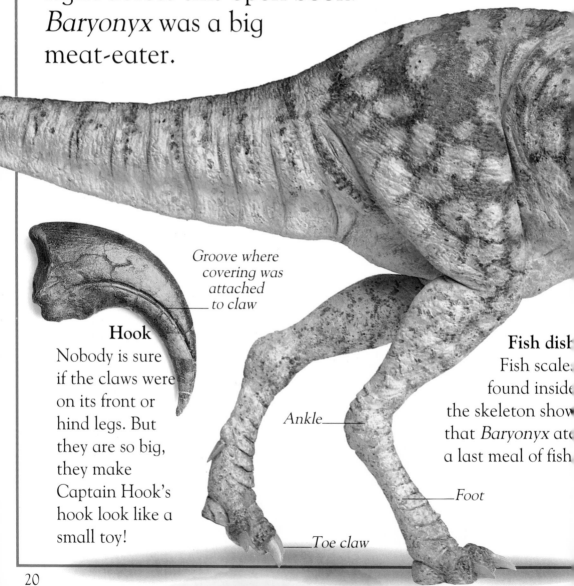

Groove where covering was attached to claw

Hook
Nobody is sure if the claws were on its front or hind legs. But they are so big, they make Captain Hook's hook look like a small toy!

Ankle

Foot

Toe claw

Fish dish
Fish scale found inside the skeleton show that *Baryonyx* ate a last meal of fish

Long jaw
Baryonyx had long, flat jaws, which remind people of a crocodile. It is quite likely it ate fish regularly.

Why did this dinosaur love to go fishing?

Toothy grin
With 32 sharp teeth to grip with on each side of its jaw, no slippery fish would have had a chance to escape.

Gone fishing
Like a bear, it waded in the shallows and hooked out its catch with its great claws.

Is this the smile of a crocodile?

21

Mean machines

Ounce for ounce, some *Deinonychosaurs* were among the most ferocious hunters the world has ever seen.

Gang fighter
Deinonychus was a pack hunter. Though small, it could kill much bigger dinosaurs by attacking from all sides at once.

Killer jaw
A mouthful of curved saw teeth would slice great hunks of meat from an *Allosaurus'* victim.

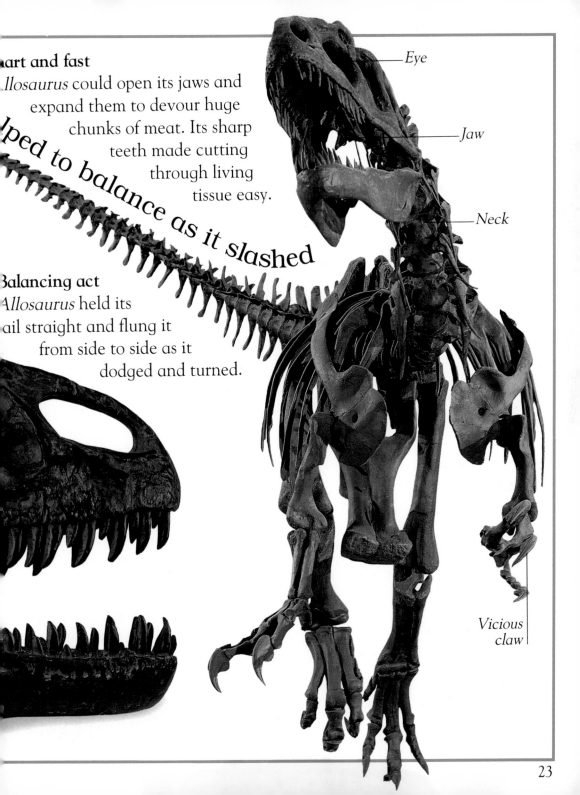

art and fast

llosaurus could open its jaws and expand them to devour huge chunks of meat. Its sharp teeth made cutting through living tissue easy.

lped to balance as it slashed

Balancing act

Allosaurus held its ail straight and flung it from side to side as it dodged and turned.

Eye

Jaw

Neck

Vicious claw

Spiky thumb

Plant-eaters all had different ways of protectir themselves from attack. In the case of *Iguanodon*, a big, spiky claw on its thumbs was used as a weapon.

A tail prop for sitting up

Flexible fifth "finger"

On all fours
Iguanodon walked on all fours with its tail held straight behind. It only rose up on its hind legs to feed or to defend itself with its spiked front claw.

g enough

uanodon grew to be 30 ft m) from nose to tail, and weighed about four tons.

Nip and chew

It had no front teeth, but used its beak to nip off leaves and twigs. The back of its mouth was full of wide, flat chewing teeth.

Beak

Thousands of bones

Iguanodon is one of the best- known dinosaurs of all. Dozens of skeletons have been found over the years.

Mandible

g mmy

needed a ge stomach and testines to digest all e food it had to eat in der to stay alive.

Foot

Mother care

All dinosaurs laid eggs. *Maiasaura* took care of her young in a nest. Here, she guarded and fed them until they could fend for themselves.

The biggest dinosaur egg were 1 ft (30 cm) long, bu most were a lot smaller.

Sometimes several females laid their eggs in the same nest.

Earth nest

Eggs were laid in a mound of earth, then covered with more soil. They stayed warm until they cracked and the babies crawled out.

Bigger than birds' eggs

Head hunter

Can you name these
dinosaurs?

1

2

3

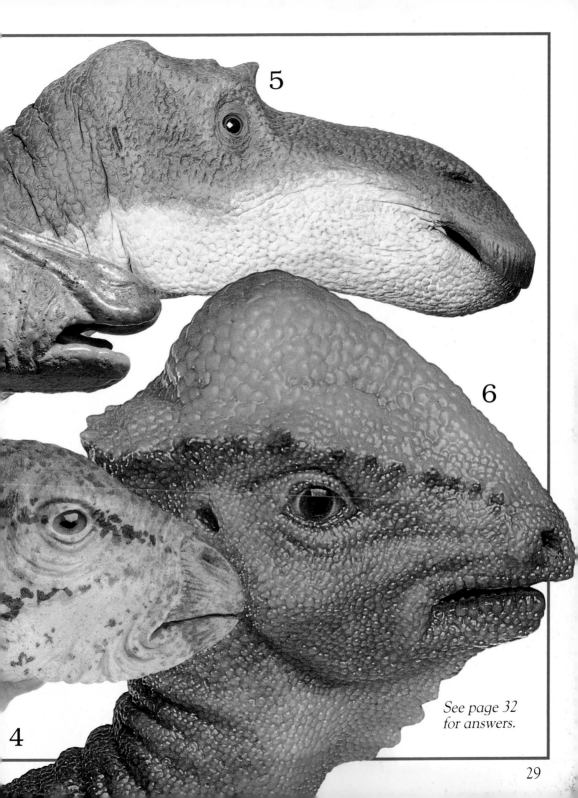

5

6

4

*See page 32
for answers.*

Index

Five fiendish questions

1) How many "fingers" did *Tyrannosaurus* have?

2) What dinosaur had plates, but never ate from them?

3) Which dinosaur could blow its own horn?

4) How did the fishing dinosaur catch a meal?

5) What made *Pachycephalosaurus* sometimes have a headache?

Answers on page 32

Answers

From page 28-29:

1. *Gallimimus*
2. *Troodon*
3. *Corythosaurus*
4. *Hypsilophodon*
5. *Iguanodon*
6. *Stegoceras*

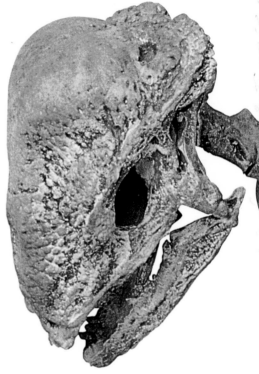

From page 30:

1. Two
2. *Stegosaurus*
3. *Parasaurolophus*
4. With its big hooked claw
5. A head-butting fight with another *Pachycephalosaurus*